FISHING FOR A LAUGH

Cartoons and Jokes
for all Angling Folks

by Joel Rothman

Published by:
Humor House, Inc.
Flat 1
12 Ornan Road
Belsize Park
London, NW3 4PX
England

Phone: (44) 207-431-0873
Email: joelrothman@btconnect.com

ISBN: 978-1-930596-53-7

Distributed by:
The Guest Cottage, Inc
8821 Hwy 47
P.O. Box 848
Woodruff, WI 54568

Phone: 800-333-8122
        715-358-5195
Fax: 715-358-9456
Email: nancytheguestcottage.com

For Lenny and Joey.

Fishing —— a sport that makes men and truth strangers.

Angler —— a sportsman that first lies in wait for a fish, then lies in weight after catching it.

How far a fisherman will stretch the truth depends upon the length of his arms.

You say you caught a
trout that was twelve
inches —— that's not
so big.

It was twelve
inches ——
between
the eyes!

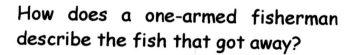

How does a one-armed fisherman
describe the fish that got away?

This is no exaggeration ——
last week I caught a fish that was so big,
when I finally pulled it out of the water
the lake went down a whole foot!

It's said that anglers sometimes catch fish by patience, sometimes by luck, but most often by the tale.

It's also said the only time a fisherman tells the truth is when he calls another fisherman a liar.

Look —— I've caught this one with my bare hands . . .

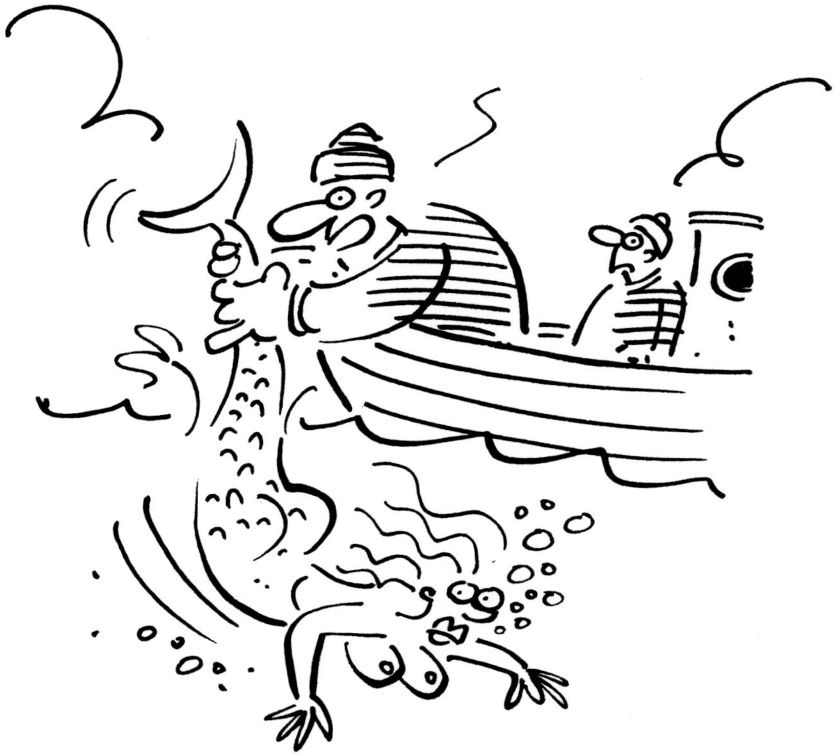

Oh give me grace
to catch a fish
so big that even I,
when talking
of it afterwards
would have no need to lie.

Do you really believe your husband
when he says he's going fishing?
He never catches anything.

That's precisely
why I believe
him.

A clergyman was strolling along the river bank with his beautiful daughter. They came across an angler and the clergyman said, "In a sense I'm also a fisherman, but I fish for men."

The angler looked at his beautiful daughter and remarked, "I'm sure you must catch quite a few judging by the bait you're using."

If fish aren't happy at
being caught, why do they
wag their tails every time
you haul them out of
the water?

Better use something else
for bait, son —— remember,
we only have two worms!

You've been pierced with so
many hooks you look like
a piece of bait.

The size of the bait
I stole was
this big!

He's got her trained right
from the start!

Just after their wedding a young couple drove off to go on their honeymoon. As they were passing a lake the groom pulled over, took his fishing gear out of the car and started walking toward the water's edge.

"What's going on?" demanded the bride. "You're not going fishing now!"
The groom turned and replied, "Are you nagging already?"

Why is it you never take me out to dinner the way you used to before we were married?

There's no point —— I don't go on feeding bait to a fish after I've caught it.

Remind me again of
how much fun I'm
having!

John and Jay were fishing from a boat on the lake. John kept hauling them in, but Jay couldn't seem to catch a thing.

"I've got much better equipment than you," remarked Jay, "but you catch all the fish."

"It's playing hunches," replied John.

"What do you mean."

"Well, when I get up in the morning, if my wife is lying on her right side I fish from the right side of the boat. If she's on her left side I fish from the left side of the boat."

"What if she's oh her back?" asked Jay.

"In that case I don't go fishing."

Ivan loves my fried salmon —
it's the second thing he'll ask
for when he returns from
the fishing trip.

Good fishing is just a matter of timing. You have to get there yesterday.

Have you noticed it's a crime to catch a fish in some lakes and a miracle in others?

It looks like he's been
waiting for a bite for
a mighty long time.

Cook a man a fish and you
feed him for a day. Teach him
how to fish and you get rid of
him for the whole weekend!

What would your father
tell you if he caught you
fishing on a Sunday?

Why don't you ask
him —— he's over
there.

What did your father say
when the fish got away?
And leave out all the
foul language!

In that case
he didn't say
anything.

I just heard about a group of Roman Catholic missionaries who were finally able to convert a tribe of cannibals. Now on Fridays the cannibals only eat fishermen.

39

When I was first married my wife made salmon all the time ——salmon salad, salmon croquettes, salmon steak, poached salmon. When spring came I had to resist an intense urge to go up north and spawn!

I'll be sure to buy some fish for your supper . . .

Step right up!
See the man-eating
fish!

45

Your husband likes to go fishing a lot.

Yes —— it's the only time he hears someone say, "Wow, you've got a really big one!"

All along a lake were anglers hoping to hook some fish. Among them was a twelve-year-old boy fishing with just a bent pin and a little pole made from the broken branch of a tree. Beside him was a large fish weighing well over ten pounds. After a while his friend came down and asked, "What kind of fish did you catch?"

"I don't know," answered the boy, "but that man over there was sure it was a fluke."

Have you had
any bites?

No, but I've
had quite a
few nips!

Look at your dad —— he went
out this morning full of hope and
now he returns full of whiskey!

Have you ever
seen a big
fishing net?

Yeah —— it's a load
of little holes tied
together with string

I heard that three
dolphin were caught
up in a tuna net
and died.

Why is there so much
concern over a few dolphin?
What about all those tuna?

I love fishing for
czardines!

Fishing is a great recreation —
it's just about the most fun you can
have with a worm on a string.

Confucius say, "Man who fish in other man's well often catch crabs."

She was a fisherman's daughter, but when she saw his rod, wow did she reel!

Penises are like fish ——
the small ones you throw
back —— the really big
ones you mount.

One question that's
always intrigued me ——
DO FISH FART?

Strange —— if I don't do anything all day I'm called a bum. If I do it with a rod by a riverbank I'm called a fisherman!

The great thing about fishing is it gives you something to do while you're not doing anything!

Two fish swim into a concrete wall. One turns to the other and says, "Dam!"

That's a nice fish you've caught!

Yes —— it certainly fills the bill!

Swordfish —— a fish with a long snout in front of him and a fishing lodge wall behind him.

You mean to tell me
you've been fishing all day
and only caught one
lousy fish?

You waited five hours for the fish to bite — can't you wait 5 minutes for me to cook it?

I once went fishing with Salvador Dali.
He used a dotted line and caught
every other fish!

Look on the positive side,
Joel —— at least you
caught something.

CARTOON/JOKE BOOKS BY JOEL ROTHMA

PUBLISHED by HUMOR HOUSE, INC.

☺   ☺   ☺   ☺   ☺   ☺   ☺

TEE HEE (For Golf Lovers)
PURRDY FUNNY (For Cat Lovers)
A PUFF AND A LAUGH
GIVING BIRTH HAS ITS FUNNY SIDE
LAUGH WHEN YOU SAY "I DO"
FUNNY HONEYMOON
THE READER'S DOGJEST
THE TAXMAN COMETH
HAVE YOURSELF A VERY FUNNY CHRISTMAS
FISHING FOR LAUGHS
THE LAUGHING KITCHEN
MISTER AND MISTRESS
OLYMPIC LAUGHS
ADAM AND STEVE
THE GARDEN OF EATIN'
CHESS FOR LAUGHS
LOVE THYSELF
A KISS AND A LAUGH
BIRTHDAY LAUGHS
LIQUOR IS QUICKER
FAT IS FUNNY